PIANO · VOCAL · GUITAR

Bruno Mars
XXIV_K
Magic

ISBN 978-1-4950-8918-3

7777 W. BLUEMOUND RD. P.O. BOX 13819 MILWAUKEE, WI 53213

In Australia Contact:
Hal Leonard Australia Pty. Ltd.
4 Lentara Court
Cheltenham, Victoria, 3192 Australia
Email: ausadmin@halleonard.com.au

Visit Hal Leonard Online at
www.halleonard.com

CONTENTS

24K MAGIC

Words and Music by BRUNO MARS,
PHILIP LAWRENCE and CHRIS BROWN

5

play- er. Look out!

Rap 1: (See additional lyrics)
Rap 2: (See additional lyrics)

(Rap ends) { Ooh, shit! } { Uh! } I'm a

Additional Lyrics

Rap 1: Pop, pop, it's show time (show time), show time (show time).
Guess who's back again.
Oh, they don't know? (Go on, tell 'em.)
They don't know? (Go on, tell 'em.)
I bet they know as soon as we walk in.
(Showin' up) wearin' Cuban links (yeah), designer minks (yeah),
Inglewood's finest shoes (whoop, whoop).
Don't look too hard; might hurt yourself.
Known to give the color red the blues.

Rap 2: Second verse for the hustlers (hustlers), gangsters (gangsters),
Bad bitches and your ugly-ass friends.
Can I preach? (Uh-oh.) Can I preach? (Uh-oh.)
I gotta show 'em how a pimp get it in.
First, take your sip (sip), do your dip (dip).
Spend your money like money ain't shit.
(Ooh, ooh, we too fresh).
Got to blame it on Jesus (#blessed).
They ain't ready for me.

PERM

Words and Music by BRUNO MARS,
HOMER STEINWEISS, PHILIP LAWRENCE,
JAMES FAUNTLEROY, CHRISTOPHER BRODY BROWN
and TREVOR LAWRENCE JR.

CHUNKY

Words and Music by BRUNO MARS,
PHILIP LAWRENCE, JAMES FAUNTLEROY
and CHRISTOPHER BRODY BROWN

*Cue notes 1st time only:

THAT'S WHAT I LIKE

Words and Music by BRUNO MARS,
PHILIP LAWRENCE, JAMES FAUNTLEROY,
RAY CHARLES McCULLOUGH II, CHRISTOPHER BRODY BROWN,
JEREMY REEVES, JONATHAN YIP and RAY ROMULUS

Half-time groove

(Ey, ey, _____ ey.) I got a con-do in Man-hat-tan;

ba-by girl, what's hap-p'nin'? You and your ass in-vit-ed, so

gon' and get to clap-pin'. Yo, pop it for the pimp, pop,

* *Recorded a half step higher.*

VERSACE ON THE FLOOR

Words and Music by BRUNO MARS,
PHILIP LAWRENCE, JAMES FAUNTLEROY
and CHRISTOPHER BRODY BROWN

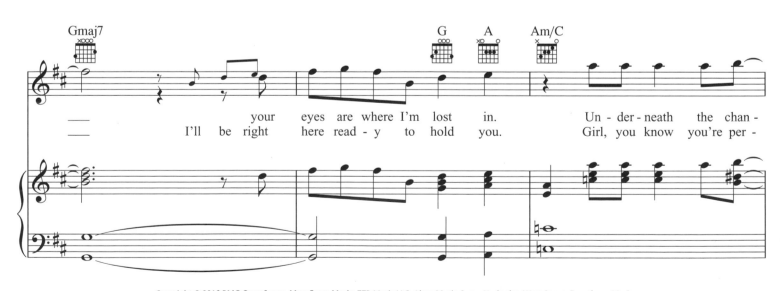

STRAIGHT UP & DOWN

Words and Music by BRUNO MARS,
PHILIP LAWRENCE, JAMES FAUNTLEROY,
FAHEE NAJM, CHRISTOPHER BRODY BROWN,
CARL MARTIN and MARC GAY

Half-time Shuffle

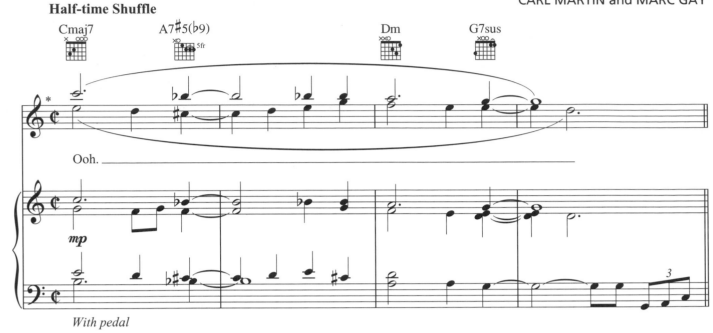

Ooh.

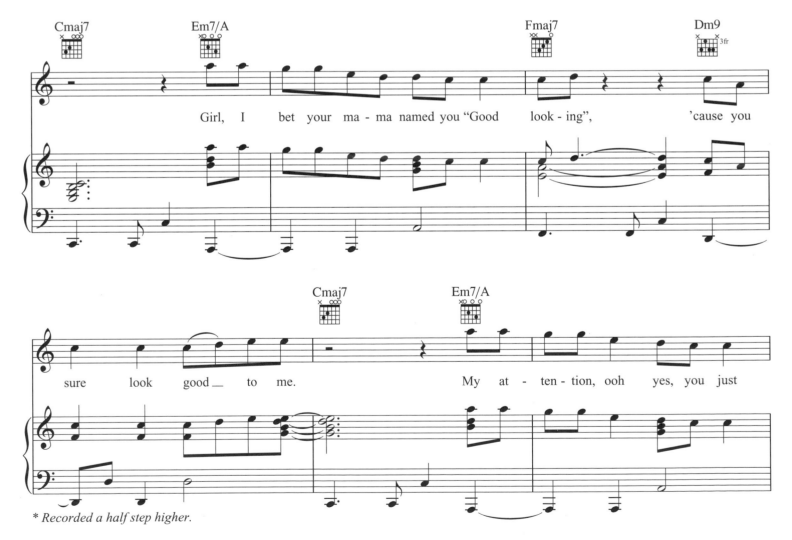

Girl, I bet your ma-ma named you "Good look-ing", 'cause you sure look good __ to me. My at-ten-tion, ooh yes, you just

* Recorded a half step higher.

Additional Lyrics

Spoken: *(Voicemail message, female voice:)* Hi, you've reached Halle Berry. Sorry, I can't get to the phone right now, but if you leave your name and number, I'll get right back to you. *Mwah!*

FINESSE

Words and Music by BRUNO MARS,
PHILIP LAWRENCE, JAMES FAUNTLEROY,
RAY CHARLES McCULLOUGH II, CHRISTOPHER BRODY BROWN,
JEREMY REEVES, JONATHAN YIP and RAY ROMULUS

TOO GOOD TO SAY GOODBYE

Words and Music by BRUNO MARS,
PHILIP LAWRENCE, JEFF BHASKER,
CHRISTOPHER BRODY BROWN
and KENNETH EDMONDS